SUPER STORIES

Kids who Became
Difference Makers

by **Amanda Hasty**

CREDITS

Copyright © 2022 by Typo Fire
Printed in the United States. All rights reserved.
First Printing, 2022

Stories written by Amanda Hasty
Edited by Joelle Worf
Cover and inside design by Kenneth Mayr
Creative direction by Robert Koorenny

Illustrations by Afzal Khan
All photos are licensed for use of this book and do not require attribution

ISBN 13: 978-0-9851702-8-8

VALUES INDEX

TABLE OF CONTENTS

HONESTY
- Chain of Conservation
- Honest Numbers

HUMILITY
- A Powerful Mind
- God's Girl
- The Champion

INCLUSION
- A Better World
- Swimming for Strength
- Together
- Your Best Self

KINDNESS
- Doing What's Right
- Swimming for Strength
- What Defines You?

OBEDIENCE
- The Misused Awl
- Waiting in the Henhouse

PATIENCE
- How Does It Tick?
- Waiting in the Henhouse

PERSEVERANCE
- Learning to Bee Brave
- Swimming for Strength
- The Misused Awl
- What Defines You?

RESOURCEFULNESS
- How Does It Tick?
- Making Flowers Bloom

SCHOLARSHIP
- Doing What's Right
- Honest Numbers
- Math in the Sky
- Your Best Self

TEAMWORK
- Math in the Sky
- Together
- When Things Change

TEMPERANCE
- Bright Path
- Finding Health

TRUST
- Finding Health
- God's Girl

HELPING HANDS

HELPFULNESS — DEPENDABILITY

What are you doing now?" Clara watched with interest as Mr. Harris worked.

"I'm grinding shells and coffee for the coloring," Mr. Harris explained, "When I work on your room, I'll grind some berries to give it a pink color."

Clara and her parents had moved into a new home. The wallpaper and paint were old, so Clara's mother had hired Mr. Harris to update the house. Clara watched in wonder at all the work Mr. Harris did, boiling, grinding, and mixing, all before it was even time to start painting.

"What did you do to the walls?" Clara moved her hand along the smooth walls.

"Before I could paint, I had to fill the cracks in with plaster," Mr. Harris explained, "I made putty and put it on the walls two days ago. Now it is dry and ready to paint."

"Is making putty and paint difficult?" Clara continued questioning.

"Clara!" Clara's mother interrupted, "Do not get in the gentleman's way." Clara stepped back and continued to watch. Mr. Harris used a large white marble slap for grinding and mixing. Clara had never seen anything like it. She wanted to know more. Clara was usually quite shy, but her curiosity got the better of her.

"Will you teach me to paint, sir?" Clara asked.

"With pleasure, little lady," Mr. Harris smiled; he had never had a child so interested in his work before. "If your mother is okay with it, I would love your help."

"Please Mom, can I help?" Clara begged, "I will do everything Mr. Harris says."

"I do not want you in the way, making things harder for him," her mother was firm, "and you cannot wear those clothes." It didn't take long for Clara to change into work clothes and quickly return to Mr. Harris' side.

Mr. Harris taught Clara how to properly hold the brushes and take care of them. She learned that it takes a lot longer to boil oil for paint than it does to boil water for cooking. As the days passed, she learned how to grind, mix, and blend the paints. When they moved to the upstairs rooms, Clara was the one who made and applied the putty on the plaster walls. She even

learned to make paste, and then trim and hang the wallpaper neatly.

"This hallway looks excellent, Mr. Harris," Clara's mother admired one day.

"Thank you," Mr. Harris replied, "but Clara did most of the work here. She has been with me every day. I half expected her to give up after the first week and return to play."

Clara smiled. She had looked forward to working with Mr. Harris each day. Even when she had blisters on her hands, she had done her best.

The day finally came when the updating was complete. Clara watched as Mr. Harris packed up the last of his brushes and buckets. She went up to her room, a light pink color now on the walls. As she lay on the bed, feeling sad that the project was over, she noticed a little box on her bedside stand. Opening it,

she saw a pretty little locket with a neat inscription that read, "To a faithful worker". Clara's sadness started to fade, she knew what to do, she would find someone else to help.

Clara Barton continued to faithfully help people whenever she could. She became known as "the angel of the battlefield" because she selflessly served as a nurse during some of the worst battles in the Civil War. In 1881, Clara founded the American Red Cross, and under her leadership it became famous for its public service and help for disaster victims.

THINK ABOUT IT

1 What did Clara learn from Mr. Harris?

2 How can you help someone else?

3 What does it mean to be dependable?

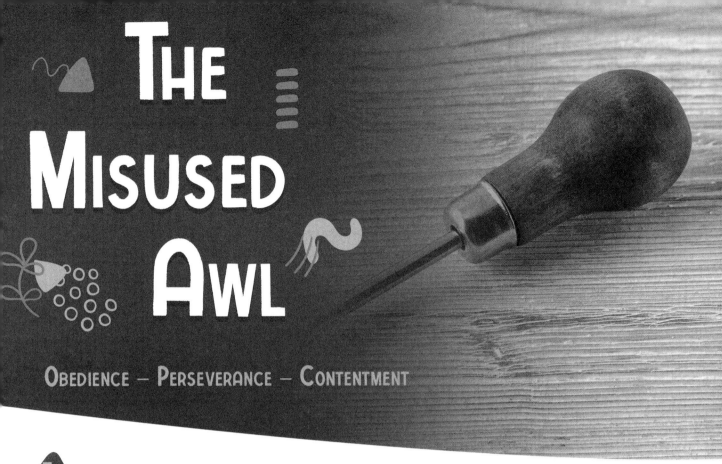

The Misused Awl

OBEDIENCE – PERSEVERANCE – CONTENTMENT

Louis watched as his dad cut pieces from the large cowhide spread across the workshop table. Carefully, he used a sharp head knife to follow the patterns. Then he turned the knife to shave the edges off of each cutout. With a lot of work, these pieces would become a saddle for Mr. Bastien.

"Louis," his dad picked up some leather scraps, "Would you like to work with these extra pieces?"

"Yes!" three-year-old Louis squealed, "I can make a harness."

Louis's dad continued to cut, stitch, stretch, and glue. It would take him many days to finish the saddle, but it would last Mr. Bastien many years. A good saddle made a long ride more comfortable for both the rider and the horse.

"Dad," Louis looked up as his dad was working on an interlocking stitch for the saddle horn. "I need to stitch my harness. Can I use that pointy tool to make the hole?"

"Are you asking about the awl?" his dad picked up the tool. It had a rounded wooden handle with a sharp metal point, perfect for making precise holes in the tough leather. "Hand your piece of leather to me. I'll make the holes, and you can do the threading." Louis's grandfather had taught his dad the craft of harness and saddle making long ago, and someday he would teach Louis. But for now, Louis was too young to use the sharp tools like the head knife and awl.

Finally, the day came when Mr. Bastien's saddle was finished. The leather was dark and shiny from the coat of lard Louis's dad had rubbed into it the evening before.

"I'd say it's some of your best work Simon-René," Mr. Bastien smiled at Louis's dad as he inspected the saddle. "It's for my new filly, she's a beauty. I brought her with me. Let's see how the saddle rests on her back."

Louis's dad followed Mr. Bastien out to the waiting horse. Louis stayed back in the workshop. If I finish the harness, he thought, maybe Mr. Bastien will want to buy it too. His dad would be so proud. He just needed a few more holes for stitching, and then it would be done.

Louis slid the stool over to his dad's workbench and climbed up. Looking at the tools spread out on the table, he spotted the awl. He grabbed its wooden handle and pushed it against his leather. Focusing on the place where he wanted the hole, he pressed the awl hard to drive the point in. In a second, the awl slipped across the tough leather, and struck his eye.

"Owwww!" Louis wailed. Falling off the stool, he grabbed at his eye. Immediately, both of his parents were running to the workshop.

"Louis!" his mother saw the awl on the floor and the blood on young Louis's face. She could guess what had happened. "Find a doctor!" She screamed as she wrapped Louis in her arms, using her apron to cover the wound.

The doctor came, but there was nothing that could be done. Louis'

damaged eye was infected, and the infection was slowly spreading to his good eye.

Every day when Louis woke up, the world looked a little darker. On his fourth birthday, he was completely blind. Louis had to learn to navigate the world without his eyes. This made everyday tasks much harder. Getting dressed, walking around the house, and eating meals took much longer, but Louis was determined to learn to do things for himself.

Using a cane as a guide, he explored the outdoors. Without his eyesight, he became more aware of the smells, sounds, and shapes around him. He learned to recognize who was coming to their house by the sound of their cart. He could tell the difference between flowers by their smell and trees by the feeling of their bark. Louis was learning to see the world in a different way, but there were still things he missed. What he missed most was watching his dad make saddles and harnesses in the workshop.

One day, Louis tapped his cane to the workshop door. As he entered, the familiar smell of leather brought back so many memories. It was his dream to be a great saddle maker like his father and grandfather, but since he lost his sight, he didn't even come in the workshop anymore.

"Louis," I have a stool for you here at my workbench. "Come sit down."

Slowly, Louis felt along the table until he came to the stool. He sat down, putting his hands on the table in front of him. He felt leather and could tell from the shape that it would be a harness. It had holes punctured along the edge, but was unfinished.

"Take these fringes," Louis could feel his dad place long, thin strips of leather in his hands. "Pull them through the holes, loop them, and pull them secure. Like this." Louis's dad held his son's hands and showed him all the correct motions. "Now you try."

Louis remembered the movements his dad had made. He pushed a leather strip through the hole, looped it, and pulled it secure. "I did it!" Louis exclaimed.

"Yes you did!" Louis's dad beamed. "Now you help me finish this one up. Mr. Bastien wants this harness by tomorrow."

Louis smiled as he worked on the harness fringes. He couldn't believe it. Someone was going to buy the harness he was working on.

Louis Braille never stopped persevering. He learned to read and write using the Haüy System, letters that were raised off of the page. The books written this way were expensive, large, and heavy. So at the age of 15, Louis invented the system of reading and writing for the blind that is still used today. We call this system, Braille.

THINK ABOUT IT

1 What did Louis's father make?

2 How can obedience keep you safe?

3 What does it mean to persevere?

Making Flowers Bloom

Helpfulness – Resourcefulness

George followed the path into the woods. The woods were full of things to discover. Every time he visited, he learned more about the plants and animals that lived there. He wanted to know the "why" of everything. What did that chipmunk chatter mean? Where was the bird going with that twig? Why did the lichen grow most on the north side of the tree? George believed that God created all of nature, and he felt that being in the woods was the closest he could get to God.

George entered a small clearing. This was his special place. Planted here were discarded flowers and vegetables, the weak ones that neighbors had cast aside when they were sick and wilting. Here, they thrived. George studied each of them. He learned what soil they liked best, and how often and when to trim them. He studied whether they grew best in the sun or shade, and what amount of water they preferred. Each type of plant had it's own special needs and George studied, recorded, and remembered the proper care for each one. He could spend hours working and studying in his secret garden.

"Mrs. Nancy stopped by while you were gone," Aunt Susan said as Ben came in to the cabin that evening,

"Remember those rosebushes beside her front porch?"

"Yes," George remembered that he hadn't seen any flowers on them this summer.

"Well, she said she thinks they're dead," Aunt Susan continued. "I mentioned that maybe you could 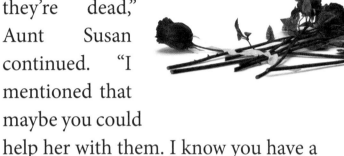 help her with them. I know you have a special touch with plants."

"Sure," George said, "I'll go visit Mrs. Nancy tomorrow after chores."

That night in bed, he thought about all the things he knew about roses. He had two bushes growing in his secret garden. He had learned a lot from taking care of them. If he cared for Mrs. Nancy's rose bushes the same way, the blossoms should come back.

The next day, when George arrived at Mrs. Nancy's house, he saw the sad rose bushes. "Good day Mrs. Nancy," George said as she came down from the porch.

"Hello, George," Mrs. Nancy smiled, "Susan said you might be able to help me with my roses. I was going to have them pulled up and thrown out. I don't

have much hope for them. What do you think?"

George crawled down to the base of one of the bushes. He carefully scraped some bark off of a low branch. Under the bark, it was green. "Well, Mrs. Nancy," George beamed, "This bush is still alive." George checked the others; all of them were sick, but alive. George started by clearing away the dead flowers and leaves at the base of the bushes. Then he pulled the weeds that were growing close by. George cut off the dead and diseased branches and watered the bushes at their base.

The next day he was back first thing in the morning with small pieces of bark and wood he had collected from the woods. He put the wood under the bushes to keep the weeds from coming back. He watered the bushes again, and then again in the evening as well. Every day he was at Mrs. Nancy's house caring for her roses.

"Welcome back Doctor Carver," Mrs. Nancy greeted George as he walked up to her house one morning.

"Doctor?" George questioned.

"Yes, you are my plant doctor," Mrs. Nancy smiled. "Look at my roses. They've never looked better. And to think, I was going to throw them out."

Around town, George became known as the plant doctor. If someone's garden, fern, or flower was sick or not producing, they called George. He was always happy to help. Every time he helped, he learned more. He found that helping others was just as much a blessing to himself as it was to those he helped.

George Washington Carver spent his whole life learning about plants. He taught farmers about crop rotation, wrote bulletins on better living, and discovered more than 300 uses for peanuts. All the things he learned, he shared freely, charging farmers nothing for his time. It is said of him, "He could have added fortune to fame, but caring for neither, he found happiness and honor in being helpful to the world."

THINK ABOUT IT

1 What did George do in the woods?

2 How can you be helpful tomorrow?

3 What does it mean to be resourceful?

CHAIN OF CONSERVATION

ATTENTIVENESS - HONESTY

Rachel and her mother took long walks in the woods behind their house. As they walked, Rachel asked questions about the plants, insects, and animals they saw. Sometimes, her mother would answer the questions, other times, they would read books until they found an answer.

Rachel also asked questions about things she couldn't see in her backyard, "What's the ocean like?" She wondered. "It's water that goes on as far as the eye can see. It's full of all kinds of creatures," Rachel's mother put a shell to Rachel's ear, "This is what the ocean sounds like." "I want to visit the ocean someday," Rachel said.

Rachel loved nature, but she also loved stories. Every month, Rachel was excited when her copy of St. Nicholas Magazine arrived in the mail. Her favorite section was in the back, where they printed stories written by children.

When Rachel was 10 years old, she wrote a story and sent it to the magazine. The next month, when her copy arrived, she saw her story printed in the back.

In college, Rachel had a hard time deciding whether to study English, to become a writer, or Biology, to learn about nature. One of Rachel's classes took her to the ocean for the first time. She waded in the water, and learned about plants and animals she'd never seen before. She fell in love with the ocean, and chose to become a Biologist.

After college, Rachel started writing about nature. She made scientific things easy to understand. She wrote for magazines, newspapers, and a government agency called The Fish and Wildlife Service.

As Rachel learned more about nature, she also learned about pollution. Big companies and cities were dumping waste into rivers and oceans, and spraying chemicals on plants and into the air.

Rachel started to ask questions, "Do humans have the right to control nature?" and "Does pollution hurt humans?" People told Rachel to be careful. She could make powerful people angry by asking questions like that.

Rachel knew she had to tell the truth, even if it made people unhappy. She wrote a book about the chain of destruction. She explained that an invisible chain connects water, plants, insects, animals, and humans. When pollution affects one, it affects them all. Her book was so popular, she was asked to speak about it on TV. The President of the United States even read her book.

Many people in big businesses and government didn't like Rachel's book *Silent Spring*. They said there wasn't really a chain, and that pollution didn't hurt humans. The president asked a group of scientists to find out who was telling the truth. After researching pollution, the scientists agreed with Rachel, and new laws about pollution were passed. Rachel Carson started a new chain, a chain of conservation.

THINK ABOUT IT

1 How did Rachel find answers to her questions?

2 How are you a part of the "chain of conservation"?
Conservation means to protect our resources.

3 What does it mean to be honest?

A Powerful Mind

'll race you to the canal," Richard shouted after a full day of work on their family ranch.

"You won't beat me," Cesar was already pulling his sweaty shirt off as he ran toward the canal.

The boys jumped in and started splashing with their cousins who were already in the water. Cur splosh! Cesar used both of his arms to create a wave in the canal.

"Ouch!" Cesar's cousin Mateo screamed, "You got water in my eyes!"

"I'm sorry," Cesar and the other children stopped splashing.

"You'll be sorry!" Mateo pushed Cesar under the water and Cesar pushed back.

"Cesar and Mateo are fighting!" Richard yelled to their mothers who were just over the bank.

"Cesar Estrada!" his mom was on the edge of the canal. "Paren Ya! Stop it now! Get out of the water this instant!" Cesar looked sheepishly at his mother as he climbed out of the canal.

"He started it," Cesar whined as he walked with his mother back to their cottage.

"It takes two to fight," his mother said firmly, "and one can't do it."

"I'm sorry," Cesar knew his mom didn't like fighting. She always told them that pushing and hitting didn't make them tough.

"Use your mind and mouth to work out conflicts," Cesar's mom continued. "In life you will meet many people who you disagree with. If you use your fists, you will both end up wounded, but if you use your minds, you can solve a problem."

"Papa," Cesar found his Dad milking the cow one warm evening. "Richard and I went to go swimming, and the canal has barely any water in it."

"Yes," his dad sighed, "It's the drought. It has not rained in a long time"

The drought continued and eventually the canal dried up completely. The fields began to crack and no crops would grow. Without money from the crops, Cesar's family could not pay the bills. They had to sell their land and find work in California, away from the drought.

In California, Cesar's family worked on other people's farms. They harvested crops like peas, avocados, and grapes. Many times they used short-handled hoes that made their backs ache, and the pesticides used on the crops stung their eyes. In the evenings, they came back to crowded, dirty camps where they lived in tents. There were no bathrooms and there was only one water faucet for more than fifty families. Because of the poor conditions, sickness spread through the camps. Some days, Cesar's entire family would only earn $0.30 for a full days work in the hot sun. When that wasn't enough to buy food, they ate wild mustard greens and caught fish in the stream.

Life was hard for Cesar's family. They missed their days playing in the wide-open spaces of their family ranch. Most days, Cesar and his siblings worked in

the fields along with their parents, but his mother wanted her children to get an education. Whenever they had a chance, she sent them to school.

"Wearing the same shirt again today?" One of the schoolboys mocked Cesar as he came in. "You probably didn't even wash it, did you? Maybe even slept in it last night." He and his friend laughed at Cesar.

Cesar could feel his face turn red. He was hot with anger and thought about how good it would feel to punch the boy in the face. Then he remembered what his mother had taught him.

Taking a deep breath, Cesar replied, "I'd be happy to wear a new one if you have an extra." There was silence for a moment. The boy was confused. He had expected a fight.

"Ummm…" the boy stuttered, "whatever…" He and his friends walked away.

That evening as Cesar lay in bed, he thought about what it meant to use your mind to solve problems. He hadn't gotten in a fight that day, and what if someone who heard him did have an extra shirt? What if he could use his mind to solve the bigger problems in his and his family's life? Did he have the courage to try? Si Se Puede. Yes, it can be done.

Cesar Chavez had the courage to start the National Farm Workers Association. His nonviolent approach made the farm worker's struggle a moral cause with nationwide support. Because of his work, conditions and pay improved for workers all across California and Florida. Cesar said, "It is well to remember there must be courage, but also that in victory there must be humility."

THINK ABOUT IT

1 What did Cesar learn from his mother?

2 How can you respond when someone is unkind to you?

3 What does it mean to be humble?

HONEST NUMBERS

HONESTY – COURAGE – SCHOLARSHIP

Bessie focused on her reader, her lips tightened as she concentrated. She had read through the stories before, but each time she understood them better.

"Time for Math," Miss Brown announced. There were only a few things Bessie enjoyed more than reading, and math was one of them. She closed her reader and pulled out her chalkboard.

"Today we will be multiplying," Miss Brown wrote the numbers 2 and 4 on the chalkboard at the front of the room, "When you multiply, you are saying how many groups you have and how many are in each group. If we have two groups, with four apples in each group, how many apples do we have?"

Bessie's hand shot up. She knew the answer.

"Yes, Bessie?"

"Four plus four is eight, so you have eight apples," Bessie smiled.

"Thank you," Miss Brown continued the lesson and Bessie drank in every word.

In August, school closed. It was cotton-picking time and every hand was needed. Bessie detested picking cotton. She would much rather be in school, reading and working with numbers, than out in the hot sun picking cotton. Bessie dragged her sack behind her; the other pickers were ahead. She pulled a boll off of the cotton plant, and separated the white cotton from the green calyx. Dropping the calyx on the ground, she stuffed the cotton in her bag. Days moved slowly in the cotton fields.

In the evening, the foreman would weigh the bags and pay the pickers for the cotton.

"Here's your pay," the foremen handed the money to Bessie's mother.

"This can't be right," Bessie's mother counted the money, "I have all my children here helping today, and this is less than I made yesterday with only a few of them."

"I calculated it out, and that's what the figures say," the foreman was firm. Bessie's mother took the money, and they started the walk home.

No matter how hard they worked, they just couldn't pick enough cotton to pay the bills. This confused Bessie, it seemed that days when they thought they had picked the most, they still didn't earn any more.

To keep food on the table, Bessie's mother spent the evenings cooking and cleaning for anyone who would hire her. With her mother gone, Bessie was the oldest at home, she made dinner for her family on the old wood-burning stove. After supper she hauled water from the well for the dishes, and then used the remaining water to mop the floors.

Before bed, Bessie would read books she rented from the library wagon. She loved learning about people in far away places. She read about Harriet Tubman and Will and Orville Wright. One of her favorite books was Uncle Tom's Cabin. Bessie didn't like the character of Uncle Tom, but she did like how the book taught lessons about treating people fairly.

One morning, before going to the fields to pick cotton, Bessie tucked a pencil and a scrap of paper into her pocket. After a long hot day in the cotton fields picking, the foreman once again gave Bessie's family less than they were expecting.

"I calculated it out, and that's what the figures say," the foreman said.

"I want to see those figures," Bessie courageously stepped up so she could see the foreman's book, "Let's weigh the cotton again." Bessie took the pencil and paper out of her pocket and started writing down the numbers and figuring out the sums.

"Your figures are wrong, Sir," Bessie announced when she finished. She held up the paper for him to see.

"I...I...I guess you're right young lady," the foreman fumbled around counting out the extra money. As he handed it to Bessie's mother, she was beaming with pride; her daughter was going to be somebody.

Bessie Coleman was the first in her family to go to University. While she was there, she became interested in flying. She saved money and earned sponsorships to attend flight school in France. Back in the United States, Bessie became famous for performing dangerous airshows. Bessie paved the way for others by becoming the first woman of African-American descent and the first of Native American descent, to hold a pilot's license.

THINK ABOUT IT

1 How did Bessie help her mother?

2 What can you learn from reading?

3 What does it mean to be a scholar?

A Cheerful Giver

Helpfulness — Generosity — Cheerfulness

As Desmond's family ate supper, his mother turned on the radio. She liked to listen to the news each evening.

"An automobile accident on the corner of Memorial and Eldon, across from the West Lynchburg Baptist Church," the Radio blared, "One seriously injured. She has been transported to the hospital and has lost a lot of blood. The hospital has asked for anyone willing to donate blood, to come immediately."

"That's terrible," Desmond's mother gasped, "We must pray for that dear woman."

"I will go," Desmond stood up from the table.

"Go?" his mother questioned.

"Yes, the announcer said she needed blood. I will donate some of mine."

"The hospital is three miles away, son," his mother reminded, "It will take you an hour just to get there. I'm sure there are others that live closer and can donate blood."

"But maybe not," Desmond insisted, "They said 'anyone willing' should come. I'm willing."

"You have a giving heart," his mother smiled, "Take this biscuit to eat on the way."

Desmond put his shoes and coat on, and then grabbed the biscuit as he left the house. It was a peaceful walk into town. The birds were singing their evening songs. The sun was painting the sky as it began to set. Desmond knew it would be dark on his walk back home, but he didn't mind.

"I'm here to donate blood," Desmond told the nurse at the front desk of the hospital, "I heard the news bulletin on the radio. About the woman in the automobile accident."

"Yes, right this way," She led him behind a curtain, to a chair. A quick prick with a needle, and Desmond could see the red blood flowing through the tube and into a bag. As the bag filled up, he thought about the woman lying somewhere in the hospital. This piece of himself might be able to save her life. Desmond smiled, just thinking of it.

As he walked home in the dark, Desmond pulled his coat tight around his shoulders. It was much colder than

he had expected. The wind whipped across his face, and he started walking faster. The birds were no longer singing, but a full moon lit his path.

The house was quiet when he arrived home. His mother sat reading her Bible by the fireplace.

"I left a plate out for you," she pointed to the table, "I thought you might be hungry. Giving blood takes the energy out of you. Not to mention the six miles of walking."

"Thank you," Desmond bowed his head before scarfing down the food. His mother was an excellent cook.

Two days later, the family was at the table again. Desmond's mother turned on the radio as they began to eat.

"The injured woman from this weeks automobile accident is still holding on," the Radio announcer informed

"Praise the Lord," Desmond's mother clasped her hands together.

him a hug as she handed him a napkin with two biscuits in it.

Desmond smiled as he went out the door, the sun painted red and yellow across the sky. Giving made his heart happy.

Desmond Doss continued to give, even at the expense of his own safety. He served as a combat medic in World War II, and was twice awarded the Bronze Star Medal for actions in Guam and the Philippines. He was awarded the Medal of Honor for his actions in the Battle of Okinawa where he single-handedly saved the lives of 75 men, carrying them back from across enemy lines, while under enemy fire.

"She is still fighting for her life, and the hospital has used all the blood that has been donated. They are asking, if anyone is willing, please come to the hospital to donate blood. In other news…" the announcer continued.

"I will go," Desmond stood up.

"You will?" his mother looked at him with a tear in her eye, "Six miles again, so late at night?"

Desmond put on his shoes. He grabbed an extra sweater before putting on his coat. He remembered how cold it had been last time.

"People like you make the world a better place to live," his mother gave

THINK ABOUT IT

1 Was it easy for Desmond to donate blood? Why or why not?

2 What makes you happy?

3 What does it mean to be helpful?

TOGETHER

"Run, Steve! Run!" Charlie yelled. Steve rounded third base and was headed home. One of the outfielders threw the ball; it was going to the catcher. Charlie held his breath.

"Yes!!!" Charlie's team exploded with excitement as Steve slid into home. They all hugged Steve at once. "Home run!" They yelled.

The summer had been filled with baseball games in the empty lot, fishing in the river, and exploration around the city, but summer was ending. School would start soon, and the boys wouldn't see each other as often. It was 1916 in Washington D.C., and schools were segregated. Although they played together during the summer, their schools separated them by the color of their skin.

Charlie's background was diverse. He had grandparents and great-grandparents who were Native American, Scottish, English, and African. He had light skin, but grew up realizing that he was treated differently than "white" children were. He couldn't go to the same restaurants or swimming pools as some of his friends. The separation was confusing.

"Why can't I go to the same school as my friend Steve?" Charlie asked his mother one day.

"It's the law," she replied, "but it doesn't have to be that way forever. People like you can change the world."

When Charlie was 12 years old, he decided to make some money selling newspapers. Every afternoon, he bought a stack of papers from the newsstand. Then he would stand outside of a big office building, and sell the papers to the businessmen as they were leaving work.

"Read all about it!" Charlie called, "Get your Washington Times and Washington Herald! Only a penny!"

Charlie sold out of his papers every day. He started wondering how many he could sell if he could stand outside of two office buildings on the same day.

So he started bringing his brother Joe with him. Together, they sold twice as many as Charlie did by himself. In time, Charlie's business grew too big for two boys, and he starting asking his friends to join them. Before long, Charlie was managing a team of seven boys. Some days, they would sell as many as 2,000 papers. Charlie couldn't believe how much his business had grown. He realized that the more people you have working toward a goal, the better your results are.

It could be the same with changing laws, Charlie thought. We play baseball together, sell newspapers together, and someday, if we work together, maybe our children will go to school together.

Dr. Charles Drew's was determined to change the world. He spoke out against racial inequalities and surpassed expectations by becoming one of the most influential scientists of the 20th century. Dr. Charles began research in the use and preservation of blood plasma. During World War II, the research of his team saved thousands of lives, and was the beginning of the nation's blood banking process.

THINK ABOUT IT

1 What did Charlie do in the summer time?

2 What are your goals?

3 What does teamwork mean?

THE CHAMPION

ATTENTIVENESS — CHEERFULNESS — HUMILITY

lec and Robert looked out over the miles and miles of land. There were few farms and no forests, just millions of purple flowers. Not many people lived out in the moors of southwest Scotland, but Alec was glad that he did. He was fascinated with the nature around him, observing and studying the rolling hills that ended at sharp cliffs, and the streams that ran into powerful waterfalls. This was their playground.

Alec and his brother Robert were meeting some friends for a rolling competition. It was one of their favorite games. The children would choose a hill and roll down it two at a time.

The person who rolled the farthest, the fastest was the winner. The winner would then roll again with another winner until only one champion was left. Today, at least ten others were coming.

"I'll go first against Oliver," Robert volunteered once their friends had arrived. Robert and Oliver lay parallel to the hill. They threw their weight towards the hill and started rolling. Arms over their heads, they held their bodies stiff. Alec watched, noticing where the ground was smoother or had a bit steeper of a slope. If he chose his spot carefully, he would have an advantage.

Finally, they were down to the last two racers. Alec and Logan were going to roll for the championship.

"On your mark, get set, GO!" Robert yelled. Alec and Logan pushed off, and were rolling fast from the start. Logan would gain a little, and then Alec would. They seemed to be going faster than any of the others before. As they neared the end, Logan pulled ahead and finished first.

"Logan's the champion!" Robert shouted. All the children cheered.

Alec was disappointed he had lost, but then he had an idea. "Let's try another hill."

"I dare you to roll down that one," Logan pointed to a steep hill that ended with a sheer drop into a canyon. Many of the hills in this area ended in cliffs that dropped down to swift-streams or whirlpools, but this one looked especially steep.

"I think I can do it," Alec headed towards the hill.

"I was just joking," Logan hesitated, "I'm not rolling down that one."

"The champion can do it," Alec called over his shoulder as he walked towards the hill. The group of children followed, watching. Alec looked at the rocks and other obstacles, and chose his route. It was steeper than any hill he had rolled down before, but he was sure there was enough space at the end to slow down. Alec lay down and started his roll. At first his body was stiff and he was confidant. Everyone will soon know how good I am at hill rolling, Alec thought.

"Slow down," Amelia gasped as Alec began to pick up speed.

It wasn't long before he was rolling and bouncing faster and faster. Alec felt the rocks in his back and he could no longer keep his body tight. His legs and arms were flapping wildly; he had completely lost control of his plummeting body.

I have to slow myself down, Alec thought. He knew he would reach the cliff's edge soon. With all his strength, Alec pulled his elbows together. Instantly he felt a shiver of pain as his left elbow collided with a rough rock, but it was just enough to turn his body and break his speed. Alec stopped just short of the cliff's edge.

All the other children were sliding down the hill towards him.

"Are you okay?" Robert called out.

Alec stood up and dusted himself off. "You all made it down as quickly as I did," he gave a weak laugh. His entire body was shaking; bruises were forming on his arms and legs. He had not paid attention to the danger of the hill, and would suffer the consequences for days.

"Are you sure you're okay?" Robert was at Alec's side.

"Alec is the new champion!" Logan announced, "He rolled the fastest."

"You can keep that title," Alec replied, "A champion should be wise when choosing what hill to roll down."

Alexander Fleming was a champion in the study of biology and medicine. His research led him to discovered penicillin, the world's first antibiotic. He was honored in 1944 when he was knighted for his scientific achievements, in 1945 when he was awarded a Nobel Prize, and in 1999 when he was named in Time Magazine's list of the 100 Most Important People of the 20th Century.

THINK ABOUT IT

1 What game did Alec and Robert like playing?

2 How should you act when someone else wins?

3 What does it mean to be attentive?

DOING WHAT'S RIGHT

SCHOLARSHIP - COURAGE - KINDNESS

Ho and his mother were poor. They lived in a basement and wore the same clothes every day. Ho didn't have toys to play with, clean water for a bath, or a bed to sleep in.

Since Ho's father had died, his mother had to work long hours sewing. Even though he was only seven years old, Ho worked hauling heavy bags of coal. After a long day's work, Ho and his mother sometimes had enough money to buy a potato to share. Ho was always hungry.

One day, a missionary offered to bring Ho to school. At school, Ho was given a clean uniform to wear, a bed to sleep in, and three meals a day. He knew that he needed to study hard. Education was his chance to live a better life.

When Ho was in his second year of high school, the students took a school-wide test. Ho studied hard, and did his very best. When the grades came back, Ho had received the highest grade. The Headmaster of the school was very proud of Ho. He helped Ho earn a scholarship to the best college in China.

Ho studied hard in college and when he was done, he took a job as a Chinese diplomat. Ho would represent China in Vienna, Austria.

Ho liked his job as a diplomat. He made lots of new friends and learned many new things. But then, the government in Vienna began to change.

One night, houses, schools, and businesses that belonged to Jewish people were broken into and burned. Instead of arresting the people that had done the damage, the government took the Jews away. Ho thought this was wrong.

The Jewish people were no longer safe in Vienna, and Ho knew he had to help. Part of Ho's job allowed him to give people visas, passes that let them leave the country. So, Ho started giving Jews visas, lots of visas.

Many people didn't like Ho letting so many Jewish people leave Vienna. Ho's boss didn't want to make people angry, so he told Ho to stop. Ho knew the Jews were not safe in Vienna, so he kept giving them visas.

One day, the government closed the building Ho worked in. So, Ho used his own money to open a new office, and continued to give Jews visas.

No one knows how many Jews Ho helped. Some people say he saved over 5000 Jews from the Holocaust. In 2000, Dr. Ho Feng-Shan was named "Righteous among Nations" by the Israeli nation.

THINK ABOUT IT

1 What was life like for Ho when he was young?

2 How can you help someone else?

3 What does it mean to be compassionate?

How Does It Tick?

RESOURCEFULNESS — PATIENCE

"Henry," it was his father calling, "time to milk the cows."

"Uhgg," Henry sighed, there had to be another way to get milk. Maybe a machine could be built to do the milking for him. Henry thought about the possibilities of machines doing other farm chores as he headed out to the barn.

"Good to see you this evening, Henry," Adolph greeted. Adolph was a German farmhand that worked for Henry's dad. Henry liked working with Adolph. While they worked, they talked about anything that had wheels, gears, or cogs.

"Did you go to Detroit today?" Henry wondered.

"As a matter of fact, I did," Adolph replied, "I purchased something special while I was there." Adolph held up a silver chain, connected to a shiny, new pocket watch. "Now I'll never be late again," Adolph joked.

"Wow!" Henry had seen a few pocket watches, but had never held one before. "Can I look at it? How does it work? Where did you get it?"

"Slow down," Adolph laughed as he told Henry everything he knew about his new watch.

The next day, after chores, Henry walked to Grimm's Jewelry Shop. He

How Does it Tick?

knew Grimm sold and repaired watches and clocks. Henry pressed his nose against the glass. Inside, he could see Grimm holding a miniature screwdriver and tweezers, he was using them to take apart a watch. It was slow and careful work, but when the customer came in to pick up his watch, Henry could see how pleased he was.

Day after day, Henry sat outside Grimm's Jewelry Shop, patiently watching him repair watches and clocks. He learned a lot from watching. Then one day, Henry's Dad came home with a gift.

"Henry," his father was clearly excited, "I have something for you." He handed Henry a small box. Henry lifted the lid, and inside he found a fine, silver pocket watch.

"A watch!" Henry exclaimed, "A watch of my very own!

Thank you!" He wrapped his arms around his father's neck.

That evening, once everyone was asleep, Henry used one of his mother's corset stays to make a pair of tweezers. Then he set his new watch on his work shelf, and carefully removed the back. He took his watch apart, the way he had seen Grimm do it so many times. Inspecting each piece, he noticed little grooves and details that he couldn't see from outside the window. Carefully, he put the watch back together.

One day after Sunday school, Henry noticed Mr. Hutching's pocket watch was not keeping time.

"I see your watch has stopped," Henry commented.

"Yes," Mr. Hutching was clearly disappointed. "I wound it up this morning, but it's still not ticking. I'll have to wait until Grimm is in his shop tomorrow to have it looked at."

"I'll look at it for you sir," Henry said. Like a professional, Henry opened the watch and unscrewed the cap covering the balance wheel. Right away he saw the trouble. Henry carefully lifted the cap over the balance wheel with his homemade tweezers and dropped it back. The roller jewel fell into place, and the escapement lever began moving. Henry replaced the screw, and the watch ran perfectly.

"Well look at that," Mr. Hutching smiled, "Someone has been studying clock mechanisms."

Henry beamed. His long hours outside of Grimm's jewelry shop had paid off; he knew how to fix watches!

Henry Ford fixed many more watches and clocks in his lifetime, but he is most famous for his innovations in automobiles. Henry used whatever he could find around the farm to make engines. After learning what he could from others, as well as many trials and errors of his own, he finally built his own gas buggy. In 1903, he started the Ford Motor Company where he mass produced cars that a working person could afford, all while paying his workers high wages.

THINK ABOUT IT

1 Why did Henry take his watch apart?

2 What can you learn by watching someone else?

3 What does it mean to be patient?

SWIMMING FOR STRENGTH

INCLUSION – PERSEVERANCE – KINDNESS

K aren's Dad blew in her face, and then dunked her under the water. Karen was young, but she had learned that whenever one of her parents blew in her face, she needed to hold her breath. They practiced breath control over and over in the pool. The more they practiced, the longer Karen could stay under water.

"Let's play a game," Karen's dad suggested, "I'll hold you back here." He stood about five feet away from the stairs at the shallow end of the pool. "I'll let you go, and you swim to the stairs."

"It's too far," Karen whimpered.

"You can do it," her dad reassured.

It took some coaxing, but Karen finally agreed. She kept her body straight and her hands over her head, Karen's dad gave her a push and she glided to the stairs.

"Great job, Karen!" Her dad praised, "Now push off from the stairs back to me."

Day after day they practiced. Karen suffered from hypotonia, or weak muscle tone. Her dad knew that swimming would improve Karen's poor muscle tone. So he gave her every opportunity to exercise her muscles in the water.

As Karen got older, she started school and her time at the pool was

more limited. One day, when Karen got home from school, she asked her mom a question, "What does retarded mean?"

"Why?" her mom was startled, "Where did you hear that word?"

"A boy at school called me retarded," Karen replied.

"Retarded means slow to learn," Karen's mom answered as she wiped a tear from her eye. It was hard to hear that someone was making fun of her daughter.

"Why would he call me that?" Karen was confused.

"You have something called Down syndrome," Karen's mom explained, "Our bodies are made up of small pieces called cells. Inside those cells are chromosomes. Chromosomes tell your body what traits you'll have, like what color your hair will be or whether you'll be a girl or a boy. Most people have forty-six chromosomes in each cell. People with Down syndrome are special, they have forty-seven."

"Special?" Karen wondered.

"Yes, you are special," her mom smiled.

"Then why would he say that?" Karen continued to question her mother.

"Sometimes people with Down syndrome take longer to learn things," Karen's mom answered, "but not everyone understands Down syndrome, and they say unkind things. It's best to ignore it, and keep going. Everyone has obstacles in life, if you find your way around them or go through them, they won't stop you."

Karen kept doing her best at school and in the pool. She was doing so well at the small pool, that her dad took her to the large outdoor pool at the Fitness club.

"Do you see the stripes on the bottom of the pool?" Karen's dad asked her as they sat on the edge. Kids were jumping and splashing, this pool was a lot busier than the small one they used to swim in.

"Yes," Karen looked at the stripes that marked out the swim lanes for lap swim.

"I'll stand on the second line, you swim from me to the wall," her dad explained. They were in the water now; kids were all around them, and bumping into them.

"I'll try," Karen agreed. The distance was shorter than what she had been doing at the other pool, but it was different here, there were so many people. Karen put her hands over her head and stiffened her body. With a push from her dad she glided to the edge of the pool.

"Great!" her dad cheered, "Now push off back to me." As he said it, a few kids swam in between them. Karen clung to the edge of the pool.

"We could stop for a scoop of ice cream on the way home," he coaxed. Karen loved ice cream. She looked around,

making sure she had, a clear shot to her dad, and pushed off.

"I knew you could do it," her dad grabbed her. They continued to practice. Karen's dad moved to the third line, the fourth and then the fifth. After many weeks of practice, Karen was swimming across the entire 25-yard pool.

"I'm so proud of you," her dad beamed as she finished a trip across the pool. As Karen pulled herself up out of the water, she saw one of her schoolmates learning how to swim with his mom.

"Did you see how Karen did it?" his mother asked him. Then she turned to Karen, "Will you show us again?"

"Sure," Karen jumped back in the water. She swam across the pool, and then back again.

"Now you try," Karen's schoolmate's mother stood on the second line, she gave her son a little push and he glided to the edge.

"Good job," Karen smiled, "I was scared at first too, but if you keep practicing, you'll be able to swim across the entire pool soon." Karen was right, it wasn't long before he was swimming laps right along with Karen. Sometimes when they came to the pool, instead of practicing, they would play games. All the kids wanted Karen on their team; she was the best swimmer at the pool.

Karen never stopped practicing her swimming, and her perseverance has helped her become the first person with Down syndrome to complete a relay swim of the 21-mile wide English Channel. She has also made the swim across Lake Tahoe, the Boston Harbor, and 16 times across the San Francisco Bay. Karen travels all over the country speaking about the abilities of people with Down syndrome. For her work, the University of Portland has awarded her an honorary Doctor of Humane Letters degree.

THINK ABOUT IT

1 How is Karen different?

2 What should you do when something is difficult?

3 What does it mean to be inclusive?

WAITING IN THE HENHOUSE

PATIENCE – OBEDIENCE – FORGIVENESS

"Danny Nutt!" Jane called excitedly. At four years old, Jane couldn't pronounce Granny, so she loving called her Grandmother Danny.

"My precious girl! I'm so glad you came to visit," Granny squeezed Jane tightly, "And who is this you brought with you?" Granny pointed to Jane's toy chimpanzee.

"This is Jubilee," Jane smiled, "Daddy gave her to me."

"Well I hope you two have fun while you're visiting me here at the farm. Maybe Jubilee will help you with some chores. You're old enough now to help out." Granny explained the different chores Jane would be responsible for

during her stay. The last one sounded exciting. "...and you will collect eggs from the hens each day. Do you understand?"

"Yes, Danny," Jane replied, still thinking about the hens. This chore sounded like an adventure.

The next day Jane and Jubilee visited all the farm animals. Jane loved watching the cow as it was milked. It seemed happy as the milk sprayed into the bucket and filled up. Jane watched the way the sheep interacted with each other. Each one with it's own personality.

When it was time to collect eggs, Jane left Jubilee in the house and grabbed a basket. She swung the empty basket as she headed to the first henhouse. The chickens pecked the ground, moving away as she approached. They were making low-pitched clucking sounds as if to say to each other, "Let's stick together."

Arriving at the first henhouse, Jane reached in and collected the eggs. They were all different colors and sizes. They were beautiful. Some eggs were large and others small; some were brown and others white. Jane wondered, How does a hen lay an egg? It didn't seem like anyone had explained this to her.

As the days went by, Jane became more and more puzzled. Every day there were more eggs, but she never saw a hen laying one. Finally, one day during chores, Jane decided to solve this mystery. She crawled into an empty henhouse and waited. It took a long time, but Jane was willing to wait. She knew that if she was going to figure out

this mystery of egg laying, she would have to be patient.

After a few hours of waiting, a hen came in. Jane waited quietly in the corner. Peeking out from under some straw, she watched the hen scratch about and settle on her little nest. Jane looked on intently as the hen half stood. She could see a little white object coming out from the feathers between the hen's legs. With a plop, the fresh white egg dropped into the straw. The hen crackled loudly, very pleased with herself. She nudged the egg with her beak and left the henhouse. The feeling of amazement set over Jane. She just saw something special.

Quickly she squeezed out of the henhouse leaving her basket behind. She was so excited to te ll her mother about what she had learned that she barely noticed it was now dark outside. "Mum!" Jane called excitedly, racing to the house.

Her mother came around the corner. "Where have you been Jane? I was scared I'd lost you!" Jane could see the relief on her mother's face as she pulled Jane into a long hug. Looking around, Jane noticed that everyone had been searching for her. Even the police had been called. Jane had been gone so long, and no one had known where she was.

"I'm sorry, Mum," Jane said sheepishly. She realized what trouble she had caused. "I was learning how a hen lays eggs." Jane's mother noticed the twinkling in Jane's eyes. They sat down together and Jane explained all that she had learned.

Jane learned two lessons that day. The first, how a hen lays an egg; and the second, to always let her mom know where she is.

Jane Goodall never lost her love of animals. Maybe inspired by Jubilee, she spent more than fifty-five years studying chimpanzees in southeastern Africa. She fell in love with them as she studied their social and family interactions. She cares for all types of animals and has worked with conservation and animal welfare.

THINK ABOUT IT

1 What did Jane learn at Granny's farm?

2 What adventures have you been on that required you to be patient?

3 What does it mean to be obedient?

WHEN THINGS CHANGE

TEAMWORK – DETERMINATION – ADAPTABLE

Rick had been fishing as long as he could remember. His dad taught him how to cast a spinning reel when he was only three years old. He'd practiced his timing so he knew when to let the fishing line go and when to lock it with the crank. His mom said that by the time he was six, he was casting as well as his dad. Rick loved fishing.

Today, Rick's Dad was taking Rick and his brother Brad fishing. They were going to a place on the Thompson River where they had been many times before, but this time was different.

Last year, Rick was in a car accident. He had been riding in the back of a truck on the way home from a fishing trip. The driver took a turn too sharp, and the truck started to roll. Rick was thrown from the truck, a toolbox landed on his back. He was rushed to the hospital where he had surgeries and months of physical therapy. Rick was stronger now, but he would never walk unassisted again. Today was his first fishing trip since the accident.

As his dad parked the truck, Rick looked at the old swinging bridge he had crossed so many times before. He remembered running and playing on it. Now, his stomach turned a little as he thought about crossing it. He knew it wouldn't be easy.

"Do you want me to carry you?" Rick's dad swung open the truck door.

"No," Rick grunted, "I can do it myself." Rick began to strap his braces on his legs. His physical therapist had taught him how to use the braces. He was faster in a wheel chair, but with the braces, he could go places the wheel chair couldn't.

With both of his legs in braces and a crutch on each side, Rick set his feet on the ground. Using the braces was a balancing act. He'd lean on the crutches while swinging one leg forward, move a crutch, then swing the other leg.

"I've got the gear and poles," Brad called as he headed towards the bridge. By the time Rick had gone two paces, Brad was already on the other side.

"Are you sure you don't want help?" his dad asked again.

"No!" Rick was firm, "I've got this."

"Ok," his dad stepped back, "I'm here if you change your mind."

Rick pulled himself up to the bridge. It was swaying, and his legs started to slide. The movement threw his balance off and BAM! Rick was on his back. His dad leaned in to help him up.

"I've got it!" Rick yelled. He knew he could do this on his own.

Rick grabbed the railing and pulled himself up. He started again, slower this time. The river flowed quickly under the bridge. Rick could see it clearly through the knotholes and rotting planks.

Left crutch…right leg…right crutch…left leg…every muscle in Rick's arms was tight. He thought about all the other times they had come here to go fishing. How he and Brad would race to the bank. How he used to carry his own fishing pole and tackle box. Rick wanted to show everyone that he could still do it on his own, but it was hard just to move himself, he needed Brad and his dad's help carry his gear. Left crutch…right leg…right crutch… left leg…he was passed the halfway point and headed back up. Rick's arms were burning now, but he had to keep his muscles tight. He could feel his legs sliding. BAM! He was on his back again.

"You've got this," his dad called from behind.

Rick grabbed the railing again, it took everything he had to pull himself up again, but he was almost there.

"Come on," Brad was just a few steps in front of him now.

Rick gritted his teeth and swung his legs, "I made it!" He yelled as he collapsed on the ground in front of Brad. His dad ran across the bridge, in seconds he covered the distance that it had taken Rick twenty minutes to go.

"Way to go, son!" his dad gave him a high-five.

Rick's smile faded as he looked down the bank. It was a steep drop down to the ledge where they would sit and fish. Before the accident, he would slide down, using the trees to slow himself. Rick looked at his legs and braces.

"Dad," he turned, "I can't do it by myself."

"We'll do it together," Rick's dad came on one side, and Brad came on the other. Holding Rick's arms around their necks, they carried him down the bank and sat him on the ledge.

"Here, put this life jacket on," his dad helped, "I'm going to tie it to the tree behind you. We don't want you falling in."

Rick felt a little silly being tied to a tree, but soon the fishing pole was in his hands. He cast the line, and pulled it tight. It felt good to be fishing again. Happy memories flooded his mind as he cast again. Rick realized, there weren't many things that he used to do, that he couldn't do again, but some of it wouldn't be the same. He just had to accept the work it took to do things on his own, and that sometimes he would need help from others. He had to adapt.

Richard Hansen never stopped pushing himself to do all he could do. He won nineteen international wheelchair marathons and became Canada's outstanding athlete of the year in 1983. To increase awareness of the need for communities to be accessible and inclusive, Rick went on the "Man In Motion World Tour". He wheeled 24,901 miles, through 34 countries—a distance equal to the circumference of the earth. His tour raised over $26 million dollars to help others with spinal cord injuries.

THINK ABOUT IT

1 How did Rick's life change after his accident?

2 How do other people help you?

3 What does it mean to adapt?

LEARNING TO BEE BETTER

COURAGE – PERSEVERANCE – ADAPTABLE

"Why do I have to go to school so far away?" Edmund whined to his mother. The past few years he had attended the local school in town, but now his parents said he had to go to a school far away. "It's so far, I'll be home late, I won't be able to go to any of the after school activities, I don't know anyone there…" Edmund listed all of the reasons why he shouldn't go.

"I want you to go to a good school," his mother patiently replied, "You finished at your last school two years early. You're advanced for your age. It'll be good for you. Now go outside and help your father."

Edmund's dad was a beekeeper, and it was time to harvest the honey. Outside, he could see his dad carefully smoking the bees. The smoke kept the bees calm.

As Edmund helped his dad, he thought about the bees. They were amazing creatures. They not only made honey, but also pollinated the nearby farms, so all the local fruits and vegetables could grow. He wished he could stay home with the bees. He was going to be a beekeeper just like his dad anyway. If he went far away to school each day, he would have less time to help with the hives.

"Ouch!" Edmund's hand felt hot where a bee stung him. He pulled out the stinger and continued to work. Edmund had been stung before, and he knew he would be again. The bees were just trying to protect their homes.

"If you get scared and start swatting them, they will feel threatened and attack." Edmund's dad always told him.

"Just be brave," Edmund told himself as he continued. "It hurts for a while, but I know the pain will go away."

A few hours later, they were done and headed in to the house for supper. "As soon as you're done eating, you'll need to get ready for bed. You have a big day tomorrow," Edmund's mother said.

"Don't remind me," Edmund mumbled under his breath. The last thing he wanted to think about was his new school.

The next morning came all too soon, and the fresh honey his mom put on his morning toast did little to cheer Edmund.

Well before the sun had risen, he was riding his bicycle to the train station. He caught the 7am train and rode for an hour and half before getting off and walking the rest of the way to school.

At school, Edmund felt small. The halls were full of students; many more than there had been at his last school. He was young and looked up to most of them. In his classes he was shy and uncomfortable. He couldn't wait for the school day to be over.

As the days went on, the long travel and the lonely school days were wearing on Edmund. He avoided sports where his size put him at a disadvantage and

he was only achieving average grades in his classes.

"Please let me quit!" Edmund was begging his mom again. "It's not for me!"

"Edmund," his mother's eyes were soft. "Have you ever been stung by a bee?"

"Yes," Edmund was confused. His mother knew how often he was stung.

"Why didn't you quit working with the bees? Surely being stung hurts?" his mother continued.

"Well," Edmund thought, "It hurts for a while, but the pain goes away. And if we stopped, we wouldn't have any honey for our biscuits."

"That's right," his mom smiled. "Many things in life are like that. Some things are hard, but if you are brave, and continue on, there is usually something sweet at the end. Here," She picked a book up off the shelf and handed it to Edmund, "bring this with you tomorrow."

The next day on the train he cracked open the book. It was about a young boy who went far away from home on an adventure.

Edmund got so caught up in reading that he was surprised when they arrived at the station. All day long he found himself daydreaming of going on adventures. He had hardly sat down on the train that evening before he had the book open and he had entered story-land again.

This became Edmunds daily practice. The long train rides became an opportunity for Edmund to travel everywhere his books would take him. He started looking forward to the ride each day, and as he read he learned new things. Things he could talk about with others at school.

School got better too. He found that he was good at boxing, and that he had endurance for hiking. His mother was right, once he had the courage to look for the best, school got a lot sweeter.

Edmund Hillary did eventually become a beekeeper just like his father. He had 1600 hives and was stung 12 to 100 times a day. He continued to read about adventures and went on many himself. In 1953, Edmund and a Nepalese Sherpa, Tenzing Norgay, became the first climbers to reach the summit of Mount Everest, the tallest Mountain in the world.

THINK ABOUT IT

1 What did Edmund learn from the bees?

2 How can you persevere when something is hard?

3 What does it mean to have courage?

MATH IN THE SKY

TEAMWORK - SCHOLARSHIP - DEPENDABILITY

"One...two...three..." Katherine counted the dishes as she set the table.
"...four...five...six..." Katherine counted the steps on her walk to church.
"...seven...eight...nine..." Katherine counted the stars in the night sky. Katherine loved to count.

When Katherine was five years old, she started school. Because she counted and read so well already, her teacher put her right into second grade. Katherine loved all the subjects, but math was her favorite.

"Everything is math," Katherine said. She added the number of words that could fit on her English page. She calculated the time between historic events in her history book. She studied the moon phases, and predicted when it would be full again.

Katherine worked hard at her schoolwork, and when she was ten years old, she was finished with eighth grade. In high school, Katherine took a new math class called geometry. In geometry class, she learned about shapes, points, and lines.

Katherine asked lots of questions.
"What are different shapes called?"
"Can you find a distance without counting?"
"How do you predict where a tossed ball will land?"
By her third year of College, Katherine had taken all
of the math classes that her college offered.

Katherine got a job working as a "computer". There were no machines to calculate numbers, so humans would write and solve long equations by hand. Her calculations helped engineers design airplanes. Katherine asked questions, and learned all she could about the airplanes the engineers

were building. She knew that when they worked as a team, the airplanes they built were safer.

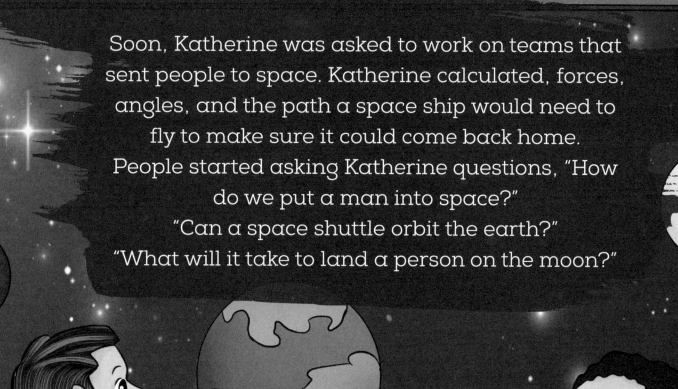

Soon, Katherine was asked to work on teams that sent people to space. Katherine calculated, forces, angles, and the path a space ship would need to fly to make sure it could come back home. People started asking Katherine questions, "How do we put a man into space?"

"Can a space shuttle orbit the earth?"

"What will it take to land a person on the moon?"

In 1970, an oxygen tank on Apollo 13 exploded damaging the aircraft. The calculations that the team had done to bring them back home no longer worked. Katherine started doing math. She worked hard and fast, writing and solving long math problems. Katherine came up with a new plan, using the moon's gravity to slingshot the aircraft back to earth. It worked! The crew made it home safe!

Katherine Johnson's calculations helped NASA on many missions. She was recognized for her work in 2016, when she was awarded the Presidential Medal of Freedom.

THINK ABOUT IT

1 What did Katherine love to do?

2 How can you learn more?

3 What does it mean to work as a team?

FINDING HEALTH

TEMPERANCE — TRUST — HELPFULNESS

"**W**hat will you have today, Johnny?" the shopkeeper asked.

"I'll take some licorice," John licked his lips, "and some sour balls as well."

"Will that be all?"

"Hmmm…" John eyed all the sugarcoated delicacies. "I'll come back for some lemon drops after work." He bit into a sweet licorice rope as he walked away.

It wasn't long before the day was over and John was eating another bag of candy on the way home. John worked for his father making brooms. Bending over the workbench hurt John's back,

but he enjoyed having his own money to spend.

That night for dinner, John had three servings of fried pork. He ate it with bread generously slathered with butter. After dinner, John had two helpings of dessert. His mom always made such good food.

Crawling into bed that night, John's stomach gurgled. He quickly ran to the toilet, he wasn't feeling well. It was a restless night of sleep, John tossed and turned, his stomach was aching. The next morning he was feeling even worse.

"Are you alright son," his mother felt his head, "You look pale."

"I feel terrible," John said, rolling over in bed, "I can't work today."

John's mother left the room, when she came back she had a bucket of cold water and some strips of cloth.

"Here, this will help," John's mother dipped a strip in the water and laid it on his head. She left again and came back with some hot porridge. "Try a few bites of this. The nutrition will help you gain strength."

After a day of his mother's nursing, John's stomach was feeling better, but he was disappointed in himself. He had missed work and the pay that came with it, because he wasn't careful about what he ate.

Later that year, John started feeling sick again. He had a fever, and was coughing. His nose was running and his eyes itched. It wasn't long before his brothers and sisters were also sick in bed.

"Mom," John coughed, "What about the cold water wraps you used when I was sick last time. I know this sickness is different, but I think they will help."

His mother brought some cold water and strips of cloth. She put the cold wraps on John and his siblings and then knelt beside their beds to pray. John's mother had heard of other families with this disease. It was called measles, and she knew that people had died from it.

Again, John's mother brought a bucket of cold water, put the cold wraps on her children, and knelt beside them to pray. John could tell how tired she was. She hadn't been sleeping.

"Let me help Mom," John sat up and took the wraps from her, "I'm feeling some better. Let me wrap Will and Clara."

"Are you sure you're feeling well enough?" John's mother felt his head and neck.

"Yes, Mother, let me help," John started using the cold wraps on his siblings.

For days John and his mother worked side-by-side, trying to bring the children's fevers down. Finally, almost two weeks after John first became sick, everyone in the house began to feel better.

As John was putting the wraps away, he passed his mother's room. He expected her to be sleeping; it had been a long time since she had had a good nights rest. Instead, he heard her speaking, praying.

"Thank you Lord for giving me the lives of my children," she was crying as she spoke.

John quietly entered her room and knelt on the floor beside her. He felt his mother's hand settle on his head.

"Lord, thank you for my son John. He ministered to his siblings when they needed him most. I pray that my son John will live his life in Your service. That he will always be a blessing to people around him."

John felt a tear on his own cheek. He determined at that moment, that no matter what, he would live his life in service to others.

Dr. John Harvey Kellogg made it his life work to help others by treating

and teaching the prevention of illness. A nutritious breakfast was important to Dr. Kellogg, and he became most famous for his work with his brother Will, inventing breakfast cereal corn flakes. However, Dr. Kellogg was most proud of his work at the Battle Creek Sanitarium. There he taught nutrition, serving low sugar, vegetarian food in the cafeteria. He also taught principles he had learned from his mother like hydrotherapy, exercise, and the value of fresh air and sunlight. His lessons on wellness became so popular that President Taft, Amelia Earhart, Sojourner Truth, and many others traveled across the country to learn from him.

THINK ABOUT IT

1 How did John help his siblings?

2 What do you do to stay healthy?

3 What does it mean to be temperate?

Artist's Hands

Attentiveness — Contentment

Maya and Tan raced into their father's studio. School was over for the day, and they spent every afternoon at the university where both their mother and father worked. Their mother was a poet, and their father the Dean of the College of Fine Arts.

Maya dropped her bag on the floor and rushed over to where her dad was working at a potter's wheel.

"What are you making?" Maya asked.

"A pot," her father's delicate hands moved slowly, forming the clay as the wheel spun. Maya watched as her father pulled the clay up, forming a pot as tall as his arm. It seemed that a single touch could open and close the shape. Although the wheel spun, the clay didn't seem to move. He pushed, pulled, and cut it with a wire. Without any effort, he formed the pot.

Maya loved studying her father as he worked. His graceful hands seemed to glide across the clay, turning a wet ball into something beautiful.

Maya had tried forming a pot, but no matter how hard she tried, it always seemed to turn out wrong.

"My hands don't work," Maya said one day while working next to her father. Her clay was a wet mass instead of a tall smooth pot like her fathers.

"You have my hands, artist's hands," her father smiled. "Art takes many forms. Be happy for the creation you made today, and look forward to the one you will make tomorrow."

Were her hands really like his graceful, effortless hands? Maya looked at her hands, and then her wet mass of clay. It didn't look like much of a creation to her. Her hands certainly didn't seem to work like her father's.

That evening after supper, Maya and Tan went outside behind their house. While Tan searched for grasshoppers, Maya sat by a tree. She watched the squirrels chatter with each other and scamper up the trees. The birds tweeted above, as a rabbit jumped from behind a bush.

It's like a forest city, Maya thought. The woods were full of so many creatures living up above and down below. They all had homes somewhere close by. Maya thought about what their houses might look like, how each one was unique, and then she had an idea.

Maya ran back to the house. Inside she found some discarded paper and cardboard. Armed with scissors, tape, and glue, she went up to her bedroom. With a pencil, she drew the face of a house, then the sides, and the back. She cut out the pieces and made a 3D house. Adding a roof and details, her house came to life.

Each evening, Maya built more houses, all different designs. Some houses were cylindrical, like the trunk of a large tree. Others were arched like the waves of the ocean. Her village soon turned into a small city.

"What have you been working on in your room each night?" Her mother questioned one evening.

"Yes, I've seen you have running up to your room with paper scraps after supper," her dad laughed.

"I'm building houses," Maya grinned, "I'll show you."

In Maya's room, her parents looked at the details on the houses, all unique.

"Look what your hands have made," her dad smiled, "These are beautiful. I

wonder what kind of a house you could make out of the clay in my studio?"

Maya beamed. She was happy with the houses that she had made today, and was excited to see what her houses of clay would look like tomorrow. Maybe her hands were artist's hands like her father's after all.

Maya Lin continued to learn what her hands could do as a designer, architect, and artist. Many of the buildings, landscapes, sculptures, and memorials Maya has designed, honor nature. When she was 21 years old, she won a national competition for her design of the Vietnam Veterans Memorial, in Washington D.C. In 2016, she was awarded the nation's highest civilian honor, the Presidential Medal of Freedom.

Think About It

1 What did Maya like to watch her father do in his studio?

2 What talents do you have?

3 What does it mean to be content?

IT'S WORTH LEARNING

ASPIRATION – SCHOLARSHIP – ECONOMY

I wonder what it's like to be weightless, Ellen wondered. She was curled up on the living room couch, reading her favorite book. It was a pretend story about three children traveling through space to find their father. Ellen's mother was across the room, studying and doing homework. Along with working full time and taking care of five children, she took one college class at a time, working to get a degree. "Education opens options," she would tell Ellen.

Ellen, like her mother, loved to learn. Last year, she and 530 million others, watched Neil Armstrong and Buzz Aldrin take, "…one small step for a man, one giant leap for mankind." They were the first men to walk on the moon. It was such an exciting event to watch. Ellen was intrigued and had been reading about space ever since. There was so much to learn.

At school, Ellen's favorite subjects were science, math, writing, and music. She was a good student. She had learned to work hard in her classes just like she saw her mom do. In the orchestra, she played the flute. Some students considered it an easy class, but Ellen took it just as seriously as she did her other classes. In addition to taking classes, Ellen had been hired to help in the school office. She earned two-dollars an hour assisting the receptionist.

One evening, while Ellen was doing her homework, her mom interrupted her, "Samuel's mom stopped over today."

"That's nice," Ellen looked up from her book. Samuel was a neighbor boy, a few years younger than Ellen.

"He is starting Orchestra next year, and wants to play the flute," Ellen's mom explained, "He's never played before, and his mother thinks that it would be good for him to have flute lessons this summer. She was wondering if you'd be willing to give him lessons?"

"Me?" Ellen was surprised.

"Yes, I'm not surprised she asked. You have worked hard and are an excellent flutist. Think back to the things you learned at the beginning, teach him, and encourage him to practice regularly. I'm sure you can do it. She said she would pay you $10 an hour."

"I wouldn't mind the extra money," Ellen smiled, "I'll do it."

Ellen taught Samuel how to properly care for his flute. She taught him how to hold it, and worked with him on his breathing, so he didn't get light headed. She taught him to read the notes, and soon he could play some simple songs. It wasn't long before Ellen was giving lessons to other flutists as well.

As Ellen was putting her money away one day, she started thinking about the difference in pay she received from her two jobs. What makes my work giving lessons worth more than my work in the office? Ellen wondered. As she thought about it, she realized that she had learned what to do to help in the office in just a few minutes, and the work she did there was easy. It had taken her years to learn to play the flute well, and it had been difficult. She was earning more because she had worked harder to learn the skill. Education is valuable,

she thought, A good education could take you anywhere.

Ellen Ochoa continued her education and it took her to outer space. She became the first Hispanic female astronaut, spending more than 1000 hours in outer space. She earned NASA's Distinguished Service Medal, which is NASA's highest honor. In 2013, she became the director of the Johnson Space Center, and in 2017, she was entered into the US Astronaut Hall of Fame.

THINK ABOUT IT

1 What did Ellen learn from her mom?

2 Could you put more effort into learning? If so, how?

3 What does it mean to aspire to something?

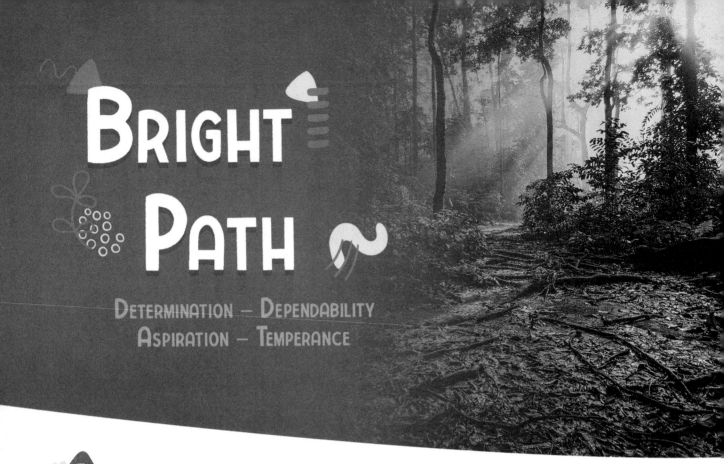

BRIGHT PATH

DETERMINATION — DEPENDABILITY
ASPIRATION — TEMPERANCE

"I'm going to catch a big one today," Charlie announced as he put his fishing line into the river, "Frank caught a twenty-pound catfish down by the falls."

"No, way," Jim blurted, "It couldn't have been that big!"

"I know it was, I helped him haul it out," Charlie insisted.

"Well, I'll catch a twenty-five pounder then," Jim smirked.

"I saw how he caught it, so I know how to catch big ones," Charlie declared, "I'll catch a thirty-pound fish."

Jim and Charlie were twins. They were almost always together, and liked to compete.

"How about whoever catches the biggest fish gets to take a marble from the other," Jim challenged, "Deal?"

"Deal!"

The boys both caught some fish, but in the end, Charlie caught the biggest one. They strung the fish up with their line and started heading back home.

"I'll race you home," Jim challenged, "If I win, I get to keep my marble, and if you win, you get two. Deal?"

"Deal!" Charlie took off, and Jim was immediately on his trail.

The boys sped out from the trees and into the open field. The house was in view. Jim gained on Charlie and then passed him. With a last burst of speed, Jim increased his lead and burst into the house, dropping his fish on the floor. Charlie sped through the doorway a second later.

"Whoa!" their mother jumped in surprise, "Looks like you boys need to clean up before supper." She brought the fish to the counter and continued cooking.

"You brought some nice fish home," Jim's mother commented as the family sat down to supper.

"Yes," Charlie smiled, "I caught the biggest one!"

"But I won the race home," Jim interjected.

"You were both winners today," their mother laughed.

"Well, fish are more important than running," Charlie declared, "Because fish give us something to eat. Right, Mom?"

"I always appreciate you bringing me fish home, but running is important too. My mother used to tell me stories of some of the great runners of our tribe. They not only had to be fast, they also had to be dependable, and smart."

"Tell us," Jim begged.

"Well, back a long time ago, Chiefs would choose fast, dependable young men to be runners. The runners would memorize messages that would sometimes take hours to tell. They would have to remember these messages for their entire run, which could be hours or days long."

"What kind of messages?" Charlie asked.

"Many kinds. Sometimes they would negotiate a treaty with another tribe, or make an alliance to avoid war. Many times they had to bring another long message back home to their own tribe. These runners were heroes."

"I could have been a runner like that!" Jim exclaimed.

"Yes, you both could have, but it would have taken training and dedication. To stay in shape, the runners ran hundreds of miles, even when they weren't delivering messages. They had to eat food that would keep their body swift, and they strengthened their mind by studying with the tribal wisdom keepers."

"Are there any more tribal runners now?" Jim wondered.

"Just a few years after you were born, hundreds of Lakota's, mostly women and children, were killed on their reservation by the U.S. Calvary.

The Calvary claimed that what they did was necessary. The Lakota didn't see it that way. Lakota runners ran all the way to Washington D.C. to tell their side of the story."

"Wow!" Jim was impressed, "I'll run to Washington D.C. if our tribe needs me to."

"I believe you would," his mom smiled, "Those runners were running for something they believed in, just like the runners a long time ago. The entire tribe was relying on them to deliver the message."

As Jim lay in bed that night, he thought about the name his mother had given him when he was born, Wa-Tho-Huk, which means Bright Path. It was a perfect name for a tribal runner. A runner whose path was lit with purpose as he ran to share a message for his people.

Jim Thorpe, a member of the Sac and Fox Nation, did run for his people. In 1912, he became the first Native American to win an Olympic Gold Medal for the United States.

The Associated Press named Jim the greatest athlete from the first half of the twentieth century. Not only did he win Gold in the 1912 pentathlon and decathlon; he also played professional football, baseball, and basketball.

THINK ABOUT IT

1 What does Jim's name, Wa-Tho-Huk, mean?

2 How do others depend on you?

3 What does it mean to be determined?

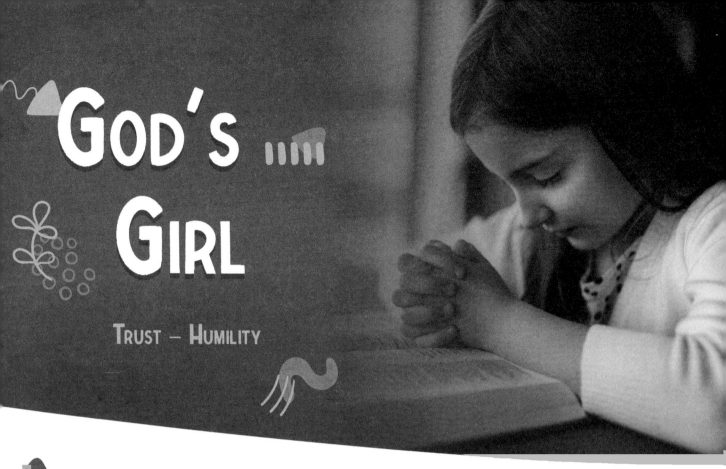

GOD'S GIRL

TRUST – HUMILITY

Lily and Jerdy warmed their hands by the fire while their parents sat at the table discussing spring planting and whether they would grow cotton or wheat in the coming year.

"The price of cotton just keeps droppin'," Mr. Mason, Jerdy's dad said, "I'd have no hope if it wasn't for the Lord. It wasn't long ago that I had no trust in Him…" Mr. Mason leaned in towards the adults, and Lily could no longer hear what he was saying. Quietly, she pulled her stool closer to the table.

"There was a camp meeting being held in a nearby town," Mr. Mason told the story of the preachers he'd heard.

How he'd walked to the meetings every night. "…and the Lord saved me," Mr. Mason leaned back in his chair as he finished.

Lily knew about God, and her family went to church on Christmas Eve and Easter, but she had never heard someone speak about God in that way. Mr. Mason spoke about God like He was a friend.

"We're holding a prayer meeting at our house Wednesday night. You folks are welcome to come," Mr. Mason invited as he stood to leave, "Children, it's late, time we head home."

Lily turned to say goodbye to Jerdy. She was listening so closely to Mr.

Mason that she had forgotten her friend was there.

"Maybe we'll see you on Wednesday," Lily gave Jerdy a hug.

Wednesday came, and Lily found her mother working in the kitchen.

"Are we going to prayer meeting at the Mason's?" Lily asked.

"I've got too much to finish here," her mother continued to knead dough on the counter, "Plus, your father is in town today, and he won't want to go back out again tonight."

"Can I go?" Lily asked. She had been thinking about Mr. Mason's words, and wanted to hear more.

"If you finish your chores," her mother replied.

Lily did finish her chores, and soon she was putting on her jacket and boots to leave. Lily took the worn path through the woods that went from her family's cottage to the Mason's.

As Lily entered the house, she saw mostly adults sitting around the stone fireplace. They were singing a song she had never heard. Lily squeezed onto the seat next to Jerdy and listened.

"…For once I was lost, but now I'm found, was blind, but now I see…" the group sang.

"Let's pray," Mr. Mason and the

others dropped to their knees, and bowed their heads. Lily copied them.

"Oh, magnificent Father," Mr. Mason began, "You have given us innumerable blessings. So many that our cup overflows." Lily had a hard time understanding the words he was saying, and the hard floor made her knees ache. The prayer seemed to last an hour, and Lily was happy when she heard Mr. Mason say, "Amen."

As everyone sat back in their chairs, Mr. Mason opened his Bible and began to read. "For God so loved the world, that He gave his only begotten son, that whosoever believeth in Him should not perish, but have everlasting life," Mr. Mason looked up and Lily could see tears in his eyes. "We just have to believe, He's done the rest," Mr. Mason began to tell the story of what God had done in his life. Again, Lily found herself lost in Mr. Mason's words, and before she was ready, he was finished.

As Lily was preparing to leave, she heard Mr. Mason call out to her. "Next prayer meeting, I'm going to call on you to pray."

"W-What?" Lily stuttered.

"You can try," Mr. Mason smiled.

Lily had never prayed before, she had never even tried.

The next day, after school, Lily took a pencil and paper, and climbed into the loft. She started writing out things she remembered hearing Mr. Mason say. Oh Lord our great Benefactor…the Great and Mighty One… Lily wrote, erased, and re-wrote her prayer. She tried to add everything she thought would impress God and the people at prayer meeting. After she finished writing her prayer, she memorized it. She wanted it to be perfect.

The next prayer meeting came, and after songs, everyone dropped to their knees.

"Lily, will you pray for us?" Mr. Mason asked.

"O-Oh, L-Lord," Lily stuttered, she had forgotten all the words, "Great, Oh Benefactor, Oh, Lord." Lily gasped, embarrassed. She looked up at Mr. Mason, and he took over.

"Lord, our Father," His prayer seemed so natural. It didn't seem written out or memorized, but the words were perfect. He was relaxed, like he was talking to his friend. Lily listened and wondered, How do you become friends with God?

On the way home that evening, Lily walked slowly until she came to an old log lying across the path. At the log, she dropped to her knees. There was no one to impress, and she had no words memorized. Bowing her head and clasping her hands, she cried, "Lord, I want to be your little girl," The words came from her heart, "Lord, if I can ever do anything for You, just let me know, and I'll do it."

Lily looked up and smiled. She felt like God was close to her. Like he was listening to her the way Jerdy did. She was God's girl!

Lillian Trasher kept her promise to God. When he called her, she left home to serve as a missionary in Egypt. While there, Lillian opened a home for orphans, widows, and the blind. She spent more than 50 years at the orphanage without a furlough, even staying through the Nazi occupation. By the time Lillian died in 1961, her orphanage housed more than 1200 children, and it still houses children today.

THINK ABOUT IT

1 What did Lily learn about prayer?

2 How can you share what you believe?

3 What does it mean to trust?

WHAT DEFINES YOU?

KINDNESS – FORGIVENESS – PERSEVERANCE

Lizzie was so excited to be starting school. Her backpack was bigger than she was, and she walked up to the first girl she saw.

"Hi, my name's Lizzie. What's your name?" Lizzie beamed.

The girl looked at Lizzie like she was a monster. Without saying a word, the girl turned and walked away. Lizzie didn't understand. She walked up to another group of students, smiled, and introduced herself again.

"You look funny," one of the children said. They all started laughing.

That was the day Lizzie learned about bullies. The kids that wouldn't let her play with them, the ones that said mean things.

"What did I do?" Lizzie asked her mom when she got home, "What's wrong with me?"

"You didn't do anything," Lizzie's mom gave her a big hug, "You have a syndrome that makes you smaller than other kids. It's something even the doctors don't understand, but the syndrome does not have to define you. Go to school tomorrow, continue to be yourself, and the kids will see that you are just like them."

By the time middle school came, Lizzie had learned to let her personality shine. She joined clubs and made some great friends. People wanted to be around Lizzie because she was fun and made them smile. There were still mornings when Lizzie would look in the mirror and wish she could scrub the syndrome off. She struggled with how she looked, but she liked the person she was, and when others got to know her, they did too.

One afternoon, Lizzie was in her room playing on her computer. She was supposed to be doing homework, but was looking for music to listen to instead. As Lizzie was scrolling, she came across a video called, "The World's Ugliest Woman." She clicked on it, and her jaw dropped.

The video was only 8 seconds long and had no sound, but it was a video of her. HER! Lizzie!? This video with four million views was calling her the ugliest woman in the world. Lizzie scrolled down to the comments and started to read.

"What's wrong with her?"

"Why did her parents keep her?"

"Put a bag over your head when you go out!!"

Lizzie knew she should stop reading, but she couldn't. There were hundreds of comments from strangers, people who didn't even know her. They were saying such mean things. Worse things than any of the bullies at school had ever said.

It was then that Lizzie looked over her shoulder and saw her mom standing there. Both of them broke into tears.

"Oh, Lizzie," her mom cried as she closed the computer.

"Mom, they're saying such mean things."

"I know honey," Lizzie's mom hugged her for a while without saying anything, "Those strangers don't define you, don't read any more of what they have to say. How about we get out of the house?"

But Lizzie didn't want to leave the house. She laid on the floor for hours, and then cried herself to sleep. The next day at school, she didn't tell her friends that she had seen the video. She was so embarrassed. When she got home, she pulled the video up again and flagged it. At least if that terrible video was taken down, the horrible comments would go with it. She cried herself to sleep again that night.

A few days later, Lizzie received a message from the person who had posted the video. She opened it, hoping for an apology. She hoped he realized that it wasn't funny, and that videos like that were bullying.

The message read, "I WON'T GIVE UP. Are you happy now that my video has been removed? I will reload it again and again and again. It's just information."

What? Lizzie was stunned. What he considered "just information" had turned her life upside down. It had brought back all the pain of her first day of kindergarten. She felt alone and exposed.

All of a sudden, Lizzie realized that she wasn't sad anymore, she was mad. She started typing a response as her dad

walked in the room. Quietly, he read the message, and Lizzie's response.

"You can't send that," he sat his hand on her shoulder.

"Why not!?" Lizzie snapped.

"He is a bully, but you are a kind person. Don't let him turn you into what he is. You have to forgive him."

"Forgive him!" Lizzie yelled, "Why would I forgive him? He doesn't care what he's done. He doesn't care about me. He has no heart!"

"Don't forgive him for his sake," her dad answered calmly, "Forgive him for your sake."

Lizzie didn't send the message, and she lay in bed that night thinking about what her dad had said. Could forgiving him really help her? Then she realized,

forgiving him meant not letting what he did define her. She could continue to be upset, or she could choose to be happy. She could spend every day thinking about the people who had called her a monster, or she could focus on her goals. It was then that Lizzie knew how she would win against these bullies. She would be happy and successful.

Lizzie Velásquez is determined to make the world a happier place. She has received over 60 million views of her anti-bullying videos, has spoken around the world about loving yourself the way you are, and lobbied for support of The Safe Schools Improvement Act. In 2015, she hosted a social media challenge for National Bullying Prevention Month. Lizzie has written multiple books including, *Be Beautiful, Be You, Choosing Happiness,* and *Dare to be Kind.*

THINK ABOUT IT

1 Why did Lizzie choose to forgive?

2 How can you make the world a happier place?

3 What does it mean to be kind?

A Better World

GENEROSITY — COURAGE — INCLUSION

Malala served tea to the men visiting with her father. Their house was always full with friends and relatives. After she poured the last cup, she lingered in the corner and listened.

"Be a lamp, or a lifeboat, or a ladder," her dad recited, "Help someone's soul heal. Walk out of your house like a shepherd." Malala knew he was reciting the words of his favorite poet, Rumi. The men told stories and discussed politics. Malala loved to sit and listen. Sometimes, her father told the story of Malalai, the great heroine she was named after.

Quietly, Malala slipped out of the men's guest room to the back of the house. Here, the women were gathered, cooking and laughing. The women and the men always visited separately. Malala lived in Pakistan, a place where women were not considered equal to men. Women did not have the same opportunities for work or school.

Malala's mom pushed back her long dark hair. Malala loved to see all the women's pretty faces. When they were with the men, they would wear veils and robes. Being in the back with the women was like seeing a whole new world.

"No matter what the other girls do," Malala once told her parents, "I will not cover my face like that." Her mother was shocked.

"She can do as she wishes," Malala's father had said, "She will live free as a bird." Malala's father cherished her. She knew that was rare for a Pakistani girl. A boy born in Pakistan is celebrated with gifts, his name is written on the family tree, but a girl is ignored. Malala's father had written her name on the family tree. Hers was the only female name on their family tree in three hundred years.

Malala's father gave her many opportunities; he believed that knowledge was the most important thing in life. Many girls in Pakistan had never been to school. Like most women in their village, Malala's mother could not read or write. Malala wanted to be a doctor. She knew she would need lots of school, and that she would need to study hard.

Malala's father ran a school for boys and girls. Malala was so excited when she was finally old enough to attend. She quickly learned how to read.

"Look at this girl," her father beamed, "She is destined for the skies!" Malala was very proud; she did her best in every class.

"What did you learn today?" Malala's mother asked her. She was always anxious to learn from Malala.

"We did math, science, history, and Islamic studies," Malala replied, "We are studying English and Urdu as well."

"You will know three languages

soon," Malala's mother smiled. She was proud of her daughter. "Now, will you take this trash to the dump for me?"

"Yes, Mom," Malala reluctantly took the bucket. She didn't enjoy going to the dump. There were rats and rotting food, it smelled bad.

At the dump, Malala emptied the bucket of eggshells and potato peels. As she was scraping out the last bits, she noticed something out of the corner of her eye. "Ahhh," she jumped back, scared it was a rat.

It was a girl, about her age. What was the girl doing? Malala wondered. She and some boys seemed to be sorting through the trash. Who would want to play in this stinky trash heap? Malala certainly didn't. She thought about talking to them, asking them what they were doing, but she was nervous. She grabbed her bucket, and left.

"Father?" Malala asked that evening after supper, "I saw some children sorting through the trash when I went to the dump today. Do you know what they were doing? I don't know them. I've never seen them at school."

"Those children are looking for anything valuable," her father answered.

"Valuable?" Malala wondered, "That's all trash."

"They find things they can clean and fix," her father continued, "They sell what they find, and then use the money they make to buy food for their families. If they went to school, their families would go hungry."

Malala was quiet for a while, and then she went upstairs to write a letter. "Thank you God for everything you've given me. Please give me the strength and courage to make the world a better place." Malala signed the letter and rolled it up. She tied it to a piece of wood, placed a dandelion on top, and took it outside. Standing beside the stream that flowed near their home, she set her letter afloat. Surely God will find it here, she thought.

As Malala walked back to her house, she thought about all her opportunities. Parents who supported her, school to attend, and the ability to read and write.

"Malala," she heard her mother call as she came in the house.

"Yes, Mom."

"We have an extra pot of rice and chicken," She handed the pot to Malala, "Will you take it to the neighbors three doors down. I don't know if they had supper tonight. We must never forget to share what we have." Malala smiled, God was already answering her prayers.

Malala had the courage to start helping people while she was still young. Even when people threatened her life, she spoke out about the rights woman and children have to an education. Her support for education has become an international movement. At 17 years old, she was the youngest person ever to receive the Nobel Peace Prize.

THINK ABOUT IT

1 How would your life be different if you lived in Pakistan?

2 What are you thankful for?

3 What does it mean to be generous?

Gather 'Round!

A good story captures your imagination.
A great one grows your faith!

Tune in to hear great stories every week at

DiscoveryMountain.com